EXPERIENCING JESUS

EXPERIENCING JESUS

TEN MEDITATIONS FOR A CHANGED LIFE

MICHAEL KENNEDY, S.J.

With CD narrated by
MARTIN SHEEN
and
JANNE SHIRLEY

A *Crossroad* Book
The Crossroad Publishing Company
New York

The Crossroad Publishing Company
481 Eighth Avenue, New York, NY 10001

Copyright © 2004 by Michael Kennedy, S.J.
Foreword copyright © 2004 by Richard Rohr, O.F.M.
Illustrations copyright © 2003 by Jose Ramirez.

Printed in the United States of America

Library of Congress Cataloging-in-Publication Data
Kennedy, Michael, S.J.
    Experiencing Jesus : ten meditations for a changed life / Michael Kennedy ; with accompanying CD narrated by Martin Sheen and Janne Shirley
        p. cm.
    ISBN 0-8245-2146-3 (alk. paper)
    1. Jesus Christ – Meditations. 2. Bible. N.T. Gospels – Meditations.
3. Catholic Church – Prayer-books and devotions – English.   I. Sheen, Martin. II. Title.
BT306.43.K45 2004
232 – dc22
                                                        2003025390

1   2   3   4   5   6   7   8   9   10   10   09   08   07   06   05   04

Contents

foreword

There have always been two major traditions in the contemplative life. The way of images and the way without images, the way of *cosa* and the way of *nada*. Finally, I think we need both, and this fine book is an example of just that. It starts us where most of us start anyway: picturing, imagining, thinking about, and meditating on. "Nothing is in the mind unless it is first in the senses," the scholastic philosophers said. Michael Kennedy and the fine professional voices on the CD will lead you into a "sensate" experience of Jesus, his life, and his message. But, I warn you, they will not leave you there.

The setting and story and situation are merely the con-text. You must listen for your own "text," you must allow it to be written within you, and then you must do the most courageous thing a human will ever do — reciprocate with your own response, your own dialogue, and your own free and honest heart. You must dare to talk back to Jesus, and to talk honestly with yourself. What else can you give Jesus except who-you-really-are? And the wonderful surprise is that is all that he ever wanted! Not a perfect gift. Only tyrants expect that. Just the giving of the gift. Which is the only delight of lovers.

Although many people think the Bible text is not "spiritual" enough, and they would prefer something like "Five Spiritual Laws," the poems of Rumi and Kabir, or the distilled wisdom of a Zen master, I am more and more convinced that there is deep and integrating genius in the "mixed messages" of most of the biblical text. It incorporates the struggle, the questions, the confusion, the human and the divine tug into the very mundane stories themselves. It is not rarefied, "pure" truth. The Bible is incarnational, enfleshed truth, just like we are. The medium really is the message. The struggle itself is the teacher, which is why Jesus talks so much about process things like forgiveness, patience, waiting, letting go, and the journey of prayer itself. Jesus is asked 183 questions in the four gospels, and I am told by scholars that he answers only 3 of them directly! He is not about settling the dust. He kicks it up.

Jesus, formed by his prophetic tradition, is not an answer giver or a problem solver, which is what the more spiritual and "pure" types want. Jesus instead leads you into the desert, onto the dilemma, with the tension of opposites, toward the cross. He knows that you can not, will not, remain there long without divine assistance. That is exactly where he wants you. If fact, I do not think we will ever understand Jesus as the teacher that he is until we recognize that pattern and plan.

Jesus created a spirituality that made prayer the main course, and not just a side dish. He offered a plan that the small self could not carry out apart from Divine Union. He made it impossible to make God into a product, as religion is wont to do. Coming from the unhindered dialogue that we call "Trinity," Jesus knew that it was all about relationship. He who sends the Spirit will not let you get to God without God. The "Son" knows that it is God-in-you that is seeking and desiring God in the first place. It is not about *you*. It is always about God. And all these silly little stories are just the staging area for that always and everywhere great event.

Jesus spirituality will never appear very "holy" or advanced to narcissistic or self-enclosed types. It all looks too incomplete, fragmented, and messy because the Union is never perfect. Jesus keeps the ego off center and even confused (a good confusion) because we are always on the way, in process, both "now" and "not yet." The ego wants conclusions, one-up-manship, answers, and the security that comes with them. We are always under the mercy and still totally in need of the mercy. We can never say, "I have it all," "I am the all," or "I am there."

So it is much easier to just be faithful to my daily twenty-five minute "sit" of not thinking (which is not a bad thing, by the way!). Any religious discipline or spiritual reading feels good and gives a certain kind of enlightened payoff (which is not bad either, but you can't stay there, which is why God stops providing the payoff after a while!) The small, insecure self wants to "feel" holy and spiritual — not knowing that it already is. Spiritually inflated people don't want to think about unspiritual things like messy folks, demoniacs, and corrupt temples. Why even bother with Jewish laws and customs and politics? Who wants to read about wars, adulteries, stupid kings, military alliances, and the exact measurements of the brazier in the temple? I would rather go to Mass every morning, preferably without lectionary, or any relevant sermon, or any human contact.

But that is exactly where we must begin, because that is how life begins. We start with anything, with seemingly silly things, insignificant facts, trivial events, small people, and ordinary stories — which are all just like me: silly, insignificant, trivial, small, and ordinary. How we do anything is probably how we do everything, so it really does not matter where we start. Finally the most concrete and the most specific carries the most all-embracing message — if you stay with it, love it, and suffer it long enough. It is the Christian way of incarnation as opposed to the common religious way of "spiritualization." It is not an ascent to "higher states of consciousness" but a descent into ordinariness, which is never ordinary again. When you taste one moment all the way through, you will see how to taste life in general. When you see one event honestly and truthfully, you begin to see for the first time.

It is at that point that God leads you from *cosa* to *nada,* from some-thing to no-thing, from images to silence, from words to experiences that are too deep for words, from concrete little Scriptures to universal wisdom, from this small story to The Story. As another fine Jesuit, Teilhard de Chardin, said, "The most personal is finally the most universal." What a paradox. A paradox that we ourselves are: one person as the way to experience all persons, my life as an avenue to all life.

Then your meditation will become quiet, non-wordy, and constant. You will move from an inner monologue to a continuous dialogue. And best of all, you will recognize that *you* are not initiating that dialogue or even creating it. It is flowing through you. It is happening in you, often seemingly in spite of you, and all you can do is say "thank you" to Somebody! You have been drawn into the flow that we call Trinity.

When the "thank yous" never stop, you have learned to pray. Or better, you have become the prayer that you always were.

Then formerly impossible advice from St. Paul will begin to make sense, because now it has happened in you:

> Be happy no matter what, pray at all times, give thanks for everything, because this is what God can expect from you once you live inside of Christ. (1 Thessalonians 5:18)

Fr. Richard Rohr, o.f.m.
Center for Action and Contemplation
Albuquerque, New Mexico

how to use this book

It is March 1, 11:00 a.m., at the Los Angeles Archdiocesan Religious Education Congress. Martin Sheen and I are giving a workshop on Ignatian Meditation and Justice. There are over a thousand people in the conference room. Usually when we think of meditation or contemplative prayer we think of a more intimate setting. But this Saturday morning we followed the same method we have used over the years, adapting it slightly for a large setting.

We first explained Ignatian prayer, which was developed by St. Ignatius of Loyola in his book *Spiritual Exercises*. In this small book, Ignatius outlines a method of prayer that activates our imagination by applying our inner senses to a Gospel passage. Ignatius believed that using our imagination in prayer — seeing, listening to, and engaging Jesus with our whole person — will help us to know and love him more. This love will then spill into our daily lives, to be men and women for others, forging into places no one else desires to go.

These meditations can be adapted in many different settings and can also be used individually as you listen to the CD or read them slowly and prayerfully.

That morning with the large gathering at the L.A. Congress we asked people to connect the difficult parts of their own lives to the experience of Jesus suffering on the cross. As each person began to feel Jesus' suffering and relate it to their own inner experience of suffering, deep emotions surfaced. God's presence became palpable. God's Spirit gently flowed through that big, once tumultuous, high-energy group.

More specifically, this is how we used the method of Ignatian meditation:

1. Mark's Gospel on the crucifixion was read while background guitar music played.

2. Putting ourselves in God's presence, we asked everyone to close their eyes. Martin began to read the meditation of Mary at the foot of the cross. We asked God to help us to activate our inner senses to see, feel, and hear Mary as she saw her son suffer.

3. When the meditation was finished, we asked each person to prayerfully make the sign of the cross on the hand of the person next to them.

4. Each person then wrote a few lines about what happened for them during the Gospel meditation.

5. They shared what they wrote with the person next to them.

Another meditation experience took place on July 1 of this year involving a much smaller group. Detention ministry chaplain Janne Shirley and I were giving a retreat at High Desert State Prison in Susanville, California. There were twelve retreatants.

What made this retreat special was that Moses, a young man who had participated in our meditation classes at Central Juvenile Hall in Los Angeles, helped give the retreat. He was finishing his fifth year of being locked up; his story is found in an earlier book (*Eyes on the Cross*, p. 193).

One of the meditations we used was "Who Enters First," which is found below on p. 105. Before we read it, Moses explained how he has used Ignatian meditation to stay close to God and out of trouble. I met Moses when he sixteen. He is now twenty-one. He will be released when he is thirty. Following a spiritual path in prison has helped him survive all these years.

During this retreat we broke up into two small groups. This is the method we used that day:

1. Moses read the Gospel passage that accompanies the meditation while background music played and a candle burned in the middle of the circle.

2. We then were asked to put ourselves in God's presence and to close our eyes while listening to the meditation.

3. When the meditation was finished, Moses knelt down and blessed the hands of each fellow inmate by prayerfully making a sign of the cross with oil on the palms of both hands.

4. We then wrote down how Jesus seemed to us and described a time when we have felt like the Gospel characters in the meditation.

5. When we finished writing, Moses took the candle that was in the middle of our circle and read what he had written.

6. After all of us took our turn, we blew out the candle.

This meditation experience opened each of us up, permitting us to fervently speak of deep feelings. The inmates were able to articulate movingly how God is somehow acting in all the painful areas of their lives.

At the end of the retreat I walked out of the barren prison chapel into the "B yard," a football-stadium-sized area full of inmates seriously working out. I observed how Moses and the other retreat participants had taken seriously the invitation to build up the muscles of their inner lives. It is fairly easy to see the results of the physical working out of the men in the yard.

It is more challenging to see the effects of meditation. For some it becomes easy to give up because meditation can seem like a waste of time.

But that day I saw clearly how Moses' relationship with Jesus has kept him alive while he lived in a very dark and violent place. If we put our eyes on Jesus, if we speak with Jesus about what is happening in our lives and what we are feeling, and then listen to him, something important happens. The choices we make and how we live change. And we are filled with a joy that sings in the heart that no one can ever erase.

acknowledgments

Our faith invites us to meet God as Trinity — as a community of sharing between persons. When we share life together in community we really do enter into the very life of God.

This book was created in a community of friends working together for peace during a time of war. Life here in East Los Angeles, like many other places, is fast and intense with its share of crises, violence, resistance, challenges, and celebrations. But in the midst of many-layered activity, we also take time to drink from the deep prayer water of the well, grounded in our life with Jesus. In our Jesuit parish, the meditations found in this book have been prayed with many times in community. The values they invite us to imitate guide us to help each other follow more faithfully the walk of Jesus.

Life is too difficult to walk alone. It is good to work, create, and pray with others. I am grateful to the friends who have joined in to create the musical chords found in this book and CD. Martin Sheen helped us with the recording of the CD found within. It was clear on the day of the recording that Martin read from a deep place inside, from his own relationship with Jesus. Martin generously recorded along with another faith-filled traveling companion, Janne Shirley.

After the recording, Arturo Laris stepped in and blended music and voices. His long hours in the studio expressed his determination to put together music that complemented the meditations.

The violin of Richard Garcia and the guitars of Arturo Lopez and Arturo Laris added to the richness of praying with the voices of Martin and Janne.

Our church is blessed with many murals of Jose Ramirez. This artist joined our community of friends and created drawings that reflect the message found in each meditation.

I am also grateful to Richard Rohr, a fellow walking companion whose commitment to contemplation and justice is beautifully articulated in the foreword.

As always Hector Gonzalez, Mike Roide, and Eddy Martinez worked the details involved in this creative endeavor.

I am reminded again that God is Trinity, a community of sharing. I am grateful to this community of artistic friends and many others who attempt to keep close to Jesus with meditation and who struggle to build a better world. Thank you.

who belongs?

(Matthew 9:9–13)

Introduction

In this meditation we see that Peter had a very difficult time understanding that Matthew, a tax collector, belonged in their group. Matthew had spent all his life exploiting the people. He represented one of the most hated persons in the society. Peter reacted strongly to Jesus' invitation for Matthew to join his group.

The Question

Jesus, in my own life I have rejected some people because they are different from me. I would like to reach out to one person that I normally reject by doing this concrete action. . . . Who will this be for me?

GOSPEL

As Jesus moved on from there, he saw a man named Matthew at his seat in the custom-house, and he said to him, "Follow me." And Matthew got up and followed him.

Now it happened, while Jesus was at table in Matthew's house, many tax collectors and other sinners joined Jesus and his disciples. When the Pharisees saw this they said to his disciples, "Why is it that your master eats with those sinners and tax collectors?"

When Jesus heard this he said, "Healthy people do not need a doctor, but sick people do. Go and find out what this means:

What I want is mercy, not sacrifice. I did not come to call the righteous but sinners."

Meditation

it was almost dark
    actually
    the most beautiful part
    of the day
we were all anxious
    to get into the city
we were hungry

jesus was particularly happy
    today
walking
    talking
    about so many things
        as if
        his heart was on fire
maybe
    after yesterday
        healing so many
i think this did
    something to his heart
        stretched it
        made it more expansive
the birds were singing
    as they flew overhead
i was glad
    to be a part of this group
the last hill
    before entering the city

there sat matthew
    collecting the roman tax
    from the poor
        rather robbing
        the poor
of all the tax collectors
    he seemed
    the most greedy
i had known him
    longer than the others
this afternoon
    one more time
    passing by his booth
he had bags of coins
    his gold chains
        abundant
jesus
    begins speaking
    with matthew
i glanced over at matthew
    he stood up
trying to figure out
    why jesus was speaking
    with him
i came closer
    jesus
    had his drinking pouch
        around his shoulder
    he poured matthew
    some water
        matthew took it

jesus saying
>matthew you look thirsty
>>would like to know
>>>if you are happy
>>>with your life?
>>do you feel close
>>>to anyone?
>>when was the last time
>>>you were happy?
i reached over
>to get jesus' attention
what was he doing
>>talking with this robber
>>>abuser of our people?
>what would people think
>if they see you jesus
>speaking with a tax collector?
matthew saying
>jesus
>i have seen you
>pass by here
>many times
thank you
>for this water
>and yes
>i am thirsty

tears welled up
>in his eyes
jesus could always
>do this
>he knew the right answers

    as if
    he could see somehow
    into the heart
but with matthew
    this is something different
    jesus
    could ruin his credibility
    with all the poor
was thinking
    maybe jesus' heart
    is getting too big
jesus
    saying
    matthew i can feel
    this thirst
        this unrest
        within you
    how about changing jobs
    and work with us?
could not believe
    what jesus was saying
worse
    when i looked
    at matthew's face
    i knew
    something had happened

jesus
    i...
    he began
    he couldn't finish
    at first

then
> yes jesus
> i will follow you
> if you will have me

jesus
> put his arm
> around matthew
>> brought him closer

a tax collector
> in our group?

i felt hate in my heart
> when i heard
> this invitation

thought i will never accept
> this traitor to our people

was so angry
> i was actually shaking
> uncontrollably
>> never

jesus embraced this worm
> i heard
> him say
>> see you tomorrow

looked
> at the faces
> of my friends
> they too were filled
> with shock
>> disgust
>> hate

it was late
    that night
    when we finished
        setting up camp
    there was a heaviness
        a nervousness
    that permeated our group
finally sitting around the fire
    knew
    it was time
    to talk
jesus began
    breaking the silence
        i could feel
        how much you disagreed
        with my decision
        to associate
        with matthew
    i can understand that
    but felt today
    that my heart
    has been expanding
    there is room
    for anyone
    who wants
    to change

but jesus...
    everyone talking at once
    telling jesus
    he was crazy
    to do this

jesus smiled
    in the midst
    of such strong opposition

at first i thought
    it would be easy
    working together
    in one unified group
we sat in silence
    just watching the flames
        the silence
        of the night
        was loud
andrew continued
    jesus
    why did you do this?
        we can't be seen
        with matthew
    do you realize
    how you could jeopardize
    everything we have been doing
        our credibility?
jesus
    looked
        at andrew
    he smiled

all night long
    going over
    the deep feelings
    of bringing a traitor
        into our group

the fire had only a few
    red embers left
    at 6:00 a.m.
early morning horizon

i never had sat
    through such intense feelings
remember
    that night so well
jesus
    said very little
    but something happened
    by the time the sun
    first appeared over the mountains
we wouldn't be the same
    after such an intense exchange
        of feelings
not sure
    what jesus actually said
not sure
    if that is what changed us
        i don't think so
rather
    it was what
    we had been experiencing
    during these months
it had to do
    with the heart

we really had hate
    in our heart
    and slowly

during the night
this stored-up hate
drained out into the ground
    around the still warm sand
    near the fire
as the sun
    rose
    the words that jesus spoke
        now do you see
        matthew really is our brother
somehow
    these words resonated
    within us
we slowly rose
    with a deeper connectedness
during the day
    we could feel a deep peace
    even though
    we were exhausted
we knew
    something important had happened
        in spite of everything
        matthew was our brother

healing

(John 5:1–9)

Introduction

In this meditation we see that Abel, a paralytic, had suffered all his life from a terrible physical infirmity. Near where Abel stayed there was a pool were some were healed. He was so disfigured that no one even wanted to touch or look at him. The first time in years someone stops and pays attention to Abel is when Jesus talks to him.

The Question

Jesus, in my own life I have suffered in many ways. Can you heal this part of my life?

GOSPEL

After this there was a Jewish feast, and Jesus went up to Jerusalem. Now, by the Sheep Gate in Jerusalem, there was a pool called Bethzatha in Hebrew surrounded by five galleries. In these galleries lay a multitude of sick people — blind, lame, and paralyzed. (All were waiting for the water to move, for at times an angel of the Lord would descend into the pool and stir up the water; and the first person to enter after this movement of the water would be healed of whatever disease that person had.)

There was a man who had been sick for thirty-eight years. Jesus saw him, and since he knew how long this man had been lying there, he said to him, "Do you want to be healed?" And

the sick man answered, "Sir, I have no one to put me into the
pool when the water is disturbed; so while I am still on my way,
another steps down before me." Jesus then said to him, "Stand
up, take your mat and walk." And at once the man was healed,
and he took up his mat and walked.

Meditation

the pool was still
    not moving
the rails supported the sick
    staring into the surface
    of the water
so many diseased
    hoping to be the first
is this only god
    torturing them more
    with this simple hope?
abel had been sick
    forever
    before he could remember
forgot
    what it was not to be sick
to be sick
    to be condemned
    to be rejected
        by god
abel lying on his back
    of all the sick
    he had been here
    the longest
        why was he even here?

many of his friends
    had died
    others had given up
why hadn't he left?
    he was not sure
    not sure at all
        but he had stayed
        in his corner
        with his routine
        his ways of securing food
the day had begun
    like any other day
    the sun was hot
    a crowd had gathered
        some were bathing
it had been a month
    since someone had been cured
abel did not think
    anything
    would be different today
        why would it?
his legs a little more twisted
    his hands
    a little less flexible
        why did this
        happen to him?
he looked about him
    soon it would be time
    to crawl to the gathering
    where his friends ate
he pulled the cover
    off himself

another day
    what difference
    would this make?
he gathered the crumbs
    from the ground
he wasn't hungry
    he never was
    but he knew
    he needed some nourishment
once more
    he greeted his friends
        they could walk
        would soon be gone
he would be left here
    with the others
    unable to walk
crawled back to his mat
    he stared up
    at the blue sky
watching the birds
    dive down rapidly
    to draw a little water
    from the pool
a shadow
    crossed his face
    abel looked up
    a bearded man
    didn't give him
    a disgusted look
rather
    he sat down
    on his mat

how are you doing today?
    my name is jesus
i was walking by
    was wondering how long
    have you tried to reach
    this pool?
why haven't you been able
    to reach the water?

jesus
    good to meet you
my name is abel
    good to have someone
    to speak with
        look at me
every time when the moment comes
    for a cure
    everyone rushes out
    and i am left here
    i can't help myself
can you believe it?
    i have been here thirty-eight years

jesus' eyes looked pained
    a deep compassion
    within him
    that was touched
    thinking what would it be like
the words
    vibrated deeply
    within jesus
    what would it be like?

how could someone
    have to endure such suffering?
what would one day
    be like?
to wake up
    feel your body
    was in prison
    normal relationships cut
hard not to fall
    into a deep pit
        of despair
what is it that
    has permitted this cripple
    to continue?

abel
    i am moved
    by your perseverance
    your life has been so difficult
what has it been
    that has kept you going
    every day?

abel
    couldn't say anything at first
    was touched
    that someone was giving him
    attention
jesus
    before i was diseased
    i would go
    to the synagogue

i remember
    as if it was yesterday
    when the rabbi
    spoke about god
i have been angry
    at god
    but i learned something
    during those years
        we are not in control
        of everything
    we think we are
i am just grateful
    to have enough to eat
i remember
    the rabbi
    speaking about
    job
    who was tested
    by god
        his whole life
        was turned into loss
        diminishment
        surrendering
        of everything

jesus
    deeply moved
    by abel's faith
        endurance
        for never giving up
jesus
    felt the long enduring suffering

jesus picked up abel
    in his arms
    and gently walked across
        the courtyard
    down the steps
    to the pool
jesus
    reached the edge
    of the pool
        forbidden hours to enter
        the surface glass like
jesus
    placed abel down
    both peering into the water

abel
    before i place you
    in the water
    could you tell me
    what one day feels like?

abel
    looked into the water
    tears dropping from his face
    unsettling the placid surface
    as pain tore into the water

i remember the first time
    i tried to get
    to the pool
        since i had to crawl
        i was one of the last

i remember
    a very sick man
    who looked like
    he would soon die
        he kicked me
        to get in front
this pain
    shot through
    my whole body
knew
    it was going
    to be almost impossible
    to reach the pool first
a young girl
    starts to yell
    as she emerged
    from the water
        i am cured
        i am cured
what has my life
    been like?
like having to endure
    the pain
    from that initial kick
        shooting pain
        throughout my body
i feel as if
    i am stepped on
    by so many
they are repulsed
    by my outer appearance

they don't know
    what it has been like
    to live so many years
        suffering

abel
    you are right
they dismiss
    have not discovered
    the true depth
    you contain within
maybe
    it is only
    those who have suffered
        so intensely
    that are the ones
    who learn to see
    what lies beneath
        the surface

jesus
    slowly lowered abel
    into the warm water
after all these years
    remembering back
    thirty-eight years ago
now
    in this moment
    feeling a lightness
    take over
still feeling the strong hands
    of jesus

being submerged
    jesus releasing abel
        under the water
        being transformed
at first
    in shock
    then joyfully
    abel slowly walked up
    those stairs
    that he had watched
    others walk
    for so many years

what the rabbi
    had taught
    really was true
    that my suffering
    had transformed me
    into one
    ready
    to be touched
    by god

now
    abel goes back to this pool
every day
    he sits
    with the most disfigured
    he tells them
    about jesus
    about what happened
    with his healing

soon
> the sickest
> looked
> for abel
> for healing
>> and for hope
>
> rather than the sporadic movement
> of water

something powerful
> had happened
> concerning
> the darkness
> in which those who suffer
>> so acutely

a healer
> had made his appearance

identity

(Matthew 16:13–20)

Introduction

In this meditation we see that Jesus lived a very intense life. There comes a moment in his life when he needs to reflect with his friends about who he really is.

The Question

Jesus, I sometimes find that it is hard to understand who you are, but I would really like to follow you more closely. Jesus, where do I find you in my own life? . . .

GOSPEL

After that Jesus came to Caesarea Philippi. He asked his disciples, "What do people say of the Son of Man? Who do they say I am?" They said, "For some of them you are John the Baptist, for others Elijah or Jeremiah or one of the prophets."

Jesus asked them, "But you, who do you say I am?" Peter answered, "You are the Messiah, the Son of the living God." Jesus replied, "It is well for you, Simon Barjona, for it is not flesh or blood that has revealed this to you but my Father in heaven.

"And now I say to you: You are Peter (or Rock) and on this rock I will build my Church; and never will the powers of death overcome it. I will give you the keys of the kingdom of heaven: whatever you bind on earth shall be bound in heaven, and what you unbind on earth shall be unbound in heaven."

Then he ordered his disciples not to tell anyone that he was the Christ.

Meditation

jesus
    felt lost
    felt lost
        in his thoughts
figuring things out
    inside
        breathing in deeply
way people
    look at me
way they respond
    to me
i really
    do not understand
reaching
    inside
    was i expecting this
    when i left nazareth?
feeling different
    at this moment
    far away
        from where
        i grew up
        what i am accustomed to
warm breeze
    touching jesus' skin
watching
    the stillness of the water
    in the distance

thinking
>   of his friends
>   of what his life
>   was like before
now
>   there is a different passion
>   flowing through
>   his veins
now
>   there is a vision
>   of a project
>   from his god
but it has all
>   happened so rapidly
feeling lost
>   jumping
>   from up high
>   falling down
>   waiting
>   to be caught
>   by his god
>   deep
asking his friends
>   to join him
>   around the circle
who do you say
>   i am?
what has been happening?
>   how do you see
>   all this in terms
>   of who i am?

they all looked
    surprised
people
    are saying all sorts
    of things
    about you jesus
    that you are one
        of the prophets
peter saying
but who are you?
    you touch on mystery
    you have changed everything
        about the way
        we see
        the one who made
        this world
    the way
    we deal
    with people
        the compassion
        the love
        that fills
        your heart
you jesus
    are the one
the one
    our people
    have been waiting for
you have been sent
    to save us
    to free us

all this whirled
    around inside
        of jesus
    to save
    to free
sitting
    around that circle
    jesus smiled
        tears
        filling his eyes

so many
    just go through
    the daily motions
it is
    as if
        they have not woken up
    as if
        they were asleep
peter you have begun
    to wake up
    you are no longer asleep
    you have seen
    a change occurring
    among the people
when i open
    my eyes
    in the morning
when i walk
    among the people
    i ask myself
    so many questions

something
    is happening
    with our people
i can feel
    this power
    it is strong
       great
who am i?
    messiah?
    savior?
these words
    are powerful
    to save?

all this flowed
    through jesus
closing his eyes
    remembering
    the moments
       this morning
       with his god
    one greater
       the one
       who saves
looking at his friends
    so many times
    feeling so weak
       so vulnerable
how was he going
    to really save anyone?
    when he felt so weak
       vulnerable

how important
    to draw
    strength
    from one greater
important
    for jesus
    to hear the words
    of how his friends see him
        as chosen
something
    important happened
    within him
    with these words
around the circle
    no one
    knowing
    what to do

jesus saying
    to peter
you have been blessed
    because
    you have been shown
    you have awoken
    to a greater reality
yet
    it is too dangerous
    to repeat
    these words
        one who saves
    the political climate
    being what it is

jesus
>   looking at his friends
am i so overwhelmed
>   by people these days
>   that i have stopped
>   feeling
>>   any intensity
>>   with my god?
it was like a jolt
>   of lightning
>   shooting through jesus
looking
>   at his friends
>   asking this question
>   am i so wrong
>   to want
>   to hear
>>   i am on the wrong path?
feeling at that moment
>   union
>>   strong
>   with his god
jesus
>   feeling
>   same feeling
>   when his god
>   spoke
>   at the river
>>   you are the one
>>   that i love
>   a feeling
>   of being connected

jesus
 was glad
 he had been able
 to show
 during these months
 his god's face
 who this one is
 showing what is
 deep
  deep within
 the heart of god

god
 i sit here
  around this circle
 look
 within myself
 see you
 but more
 feel you close
this deep mystery
 overwhelming
 your face dear god
who am i?
 one who receives
 my very life from you
god
 yesterday
 when i was surrounded
 by so many people
 you asked me
 to cure the paralyzed one

i felt you then
    but more
    god
    in that healing
    who you are
    was shown
who you are dear god
    compassion

to be committed

(Matthew 16:21–28)

Introduction

In this meditation Jesus speaks about the price of following him and how his work might put himself in danger and he might even be killed. Jesus begins to speak about his own suffering and death.

The Question

Jesus, many times I want to run away from following you. Jesus, I know that when I run away I will never be happy. How in my own life can I better follow you and commit myself in this concrete way? . . .

GOSPEL

From that day Jesus began to make it clear to his disciples that he must go to Jerusalem; he would suffer many things from the Jewish authorities, the chief priests and the teachers of the Law. He would be killed and be raised on the third day.

Then Peter took him aside and began to reproach him, "Never, Lord! No, this must never happen to you." But Jesus turned to him and said, "Get behind me, Satan! You would have me stumble. You are their King not as God does, but as people do."

Then Jesus said to his disciples, "If you want to follow me, deny yourself, take up your cross and follow me. For whoever chooses to save his life will lose it, but the one who loses his life for my sake will find it. What will one gain by winning the whole world if he destroys himself? There is nothing you can give to recover your own self.

"Know that the Son of Man will come in the Glory of his Father with the holy angels, and he will reward each one according to his deeds. Truly, I tell you, there are some here who will not die before they see the Son of Man coming as king."

Meditation

yesterday
>   i was crushed
>   with pressures
some of the pharisees
>   were present
they began to argue
>   with me
>   about what right
>   did jesus have
>   to heal
was hard to sleep
>   last night
the previous day had been
>   very heavy
>   intense
we were in the middle
>   of a struggle
>   with the powerful
they didn't want
>   the life
>   of the poor
>   to change
>   in any way

then everything
    would be forced
    to be different
so clear
    to me last night
        before
        finally falling off
        to sleep at 3:00 a.m.
    that this was
    only the beginning
    of the conflicts
the fire
    was now ready
    to prepare breakfast
the sun
    was just coming up
    over the mountains
food
    tasting good
    after such intensity
i looked
    at jesus
        dark circles
        under his eyes
    i could tell
    he too had not slept
    very well
so much
    happening
    within him
    these days

friends
    i would like
    to discuss
    something with you

whenever
    jesus
    began like this
    i knew
    it was going
    to be serious

friends
    during these days
    you have seen
        the hate
        the anger
    of our religious leaders
well when we go up
    to jerusalem this year
    they will try to kill me
i will have to suffer
    but this will not be the end
    of the story

everyone
    around in that circle
    was drawn into
        a profound place
        of fear
        and anxiety
this can't be

i helped clean up
 quickly
i needed to speak
 to jesus
 needed to change
 his mind
these days
 have been too much
 for jesus
 he needs a rest

jesus
 after we finish
 cleaning these jars
 i would like to speak
  with you

we walked to the edge
 of the lake
fishing boats
 were pulling
 up to shore
 after the whole night
 searching
we walked
 slowly
 along a deserted stretch
 of shore
was glad
 i have this time
 to give some
 good advice to jesus

jesus
    i know
    these days have been
    stressful
        but
        we won't let you
        be captured
        by those animals
we've got to get out
    of this region
    quickly

jesus
    stopped
his face
    was pained

peter
    you have been
    a great help
    during these months
you are strong
    committed
        but peter
        how can you try
        to avoid
        what must be done?
i will not run
    from pressures
    from conflicts
        that is how
        the world acts

peter
     what have you learned
     during this time
     working together?
          what?

that hurt
     jesus
     didn't stop there

peter
     my path
     is not an easy one
it is one
     that does not run away
     from conflicts
          suffering
my path
     leads
          directly
     to the center
     of darkness
     to bring light
peter
     i need you
     to support me
     not to think and act
     like the pharisees
peter
     my path
     will eventually lead to life
     of which i am committed

i stood there
    looking out
    into the lake
what jesus
    had just said
    hurt me deeply
i don't think
    i'd ever felt
    more hurt
my eyes
    filling up
    with tears
i also knew
    what jesus
    had said
    was true
i had to make
    a decision

jesus
    i was just
    trying to
    protect you
    but
    i painfully see
    this would be
    running away
    from what we are called
    to do

i felt better
    after saying this

jesus
    put his arm
    around my shoulder
        sorry peter
        if i hurt you
his eyes
    were also filling
    up with tears
felt close
    to jesus
how hard to accept
    the cost to enter
    into god's project
so easy
    to build
    our own personal kingdom
    without any cost
        or suffering
we slowly
    began our walk
    back to where the others
    were gathered

peter
    i know
    what i am saying
    is challenging
    but i need you
    to support me
        especially when everyone else
        thinks i am crazy
        because of what i do

walking
    that morning
    along the shore
    of the lake
    i began to see
    that i really never
    quite understood
    i thought i did
    but i really hadn't
this conversation
    is a clear example
    of how far
    i need to grow
        and then again
        maybe
        i will always
        be growing
        little by little
we walked
    the last stretch back
    to the campsite
        in silence
    connected
        in this web
        of friendship
            deep
            overflowing
joining
    the group
we again
    sat around the fire

everyone very serious
>they could feel
>jesus and i
>had entered
>into deep waters

one closest to jesus
>asked
>why do things
>have to be so hard?

jesus responding
>you have not understood
>what i have been trying
>to say

look around us
>in the cities
>everyone is so busy
>building up their
>own worlds
>>they continue
>>to desire to have
>>more and more

but friends
>our path is different
>it will seem like
>we will be losing
>>having less and less
>but
>it is the opposite

unless
>you can divest yourselves
>give everything away
>really be naked

you will not
　　have life
let go
don't hold on to anything
i invite you
　　to come with me
　　　　as i mentioned
　　　　at breakfast
　　we are going
　　to be challenged
　　by the established structures
　　　　get ready
　　　　for the confrontations
　　　　　　the struggles

everyone
　　around
　　in the circle
　　was listening
　　with their hearts
somehow
　　even as hard
　　as what jesus
　　was saying
　　　　he was inciting
　　　　　　fire
　　　　burning strong
　　　　moving us
　　　　to go deeper
　　　　to commit ourselves
　　　　to continue walking
　　　　　　with him

jesus you are the way
    maybe we can't
    totally
    understand
    what you are saying
but
    on some level
    we know
    you are right

we got up
    from that circle
    recommitted
        to pass through
        any difficulty
    not to run away
the power of losing
    everything
        and suddenly
        you have everything
what an adventure
    walking
    with jesus
felt like
    i was the most fortunate person
        in the world

a day's work

(Matthew 20:1–16)

Introduction

In this meditation we see that Jesus was used to manual work. During his years he experienced much suffering as he worked in various regions. Jesus witnessed how hard it was for many to have enough to feed their families.

The Question

Jesus by being a generous, giving person I know that this will lead to happiness. Sometimes I find that I am too selfish, too centered in myself. Jesus, what caring activity can I engage in?

GOSPEL

"This story throws light on the kingdom of heaven. A landowner went out early in the morning to hire workers for his vineyard. He agreed to pay the workers a salary of a silver coin for the day, and sent them to his vineyard.

"He went out again at about nine in the morning, and seeing others idle in the square, he said to them: 'You, too, go to my vineyard and I will pay you what is just.' So they went.

"The owner went out at midday and again at three in the afternoon, and he did the same. Finally he went out at the last working hour — it was the eleventh — and he saw others standing there. So he said to them: 'Why do you stay idle the whole day?' They answered: 'Because no one has hired us.' The master said: 'Go and work in my vineyard.'

"When evening came, the owner of the vineyard said to his manager: 'Call the workers and pay them their wage, beginning with the last and ending with the first.' Those who had come to work at the eleventh hour turned up and were given a denarius each (a silver coin). When it was the turn of the first, they thought they would receive more. But they, too, received a denarius each. So, on receiving it, they began to grumble against the landowner.

"They said: 'These last hardly worked an hour, yet you have treated them the same as us who have endured the day's burden and heat.' The owner said to one of them: 'Friend, I have not been unjust to you. Did we not agree on a denarius a day? So take what is yours and go. I want to give to the last the same as I give to you. Don't I have the right to do as I please with my money? Why are you envious when I am kind?' So will it be: the last will be first, the first will be last."

Meditation

would be good to take a break
        from the intensity
        of preaching
before jesus
        went to sleep
        he asked his neighbor abraham
        what time
        he needed to be at the plaza
        to get work
jesus was used to manual labor
        so many years
        using his hands

building houses
mixing materials for outside carpentry
also working at odd jobs
during the years
the important thing
was to earn enough
to buy the supplies
enough for food

abraham invited jesus
into his house
his eight children were asleep
the candle lit
the insides of his humble dwelling
he spoke about
how hard
it has been since his wife died
she had held
the family together
he barely earned enough
to feed them
he needed to be
at the plaza
at 4:00 a.m.
to make sure
he was picked
to work
or he wouldn't have anything
to buy food
they spoke
for a long time
in that room

jesus
> left the house
> at midnight
wandering
> off to sleep
>> pondering
>> the strength
>> and courage of abraham

after a few hours of sleep
> jesus
> was dressing
>> throwing water
>> on his face
he had told his disciples
> that he would be working
> in the fields
> that day

arriving
> at the plaza
>> still dark
>> tired faces
looking around for abraham
> no where
> to be seen
something
> must have happened

jesus
> worked hard all morning
> felt good the change

from the intensity
of past days
speaking
before the crowds
now sweat pouring
    down his face
listening to conversations
    as he worked
the hardships
    of the poor
    of this country
resting at noon
    sharing some food
    with the others
abraham
    arriving at this break
    he spoke
    of how his daughter
    had been so sick
    in the morning
        he could not leave
        her alone
he brought her
    to the doctor
he borrowed money
    to buy medicine
    now he was in debt
    more than ever
he would only be able
    to work half a day
        this was troubling

all he wanted
    was for his children
    to be happy
    to have their needs met
jesus
    spoke of his years
    working
    as a day laborer
    the skills he had learned
    since he was a child
    but it was so difficult
    to survive
    for day laborers
        even with a salary
        of one coin
this day
    he would send a portion
    to his mother
difficult
    to be separated
    from your family
        always wondering
        how they are doing
working
    all the time
    so the others
    can survive

all day long
    jesus listened
    to these workers

they lived some distance
    from caphernaum
    but needed to be here
        separated
        from their loved ones
    in order to find day work
they could not survive
    just farming
    their lands
jesus
    speaking with abraham
    about the loneliness
    that hangs on those
    who are forced
    to travel to the cities
    to work
abraham and jesus
    worked side by side
    all afternoon
as time passed
    more and more exhausted
    after rising so early
    they asked
    could the poor
    ever earn enough
    to find some stability?

soon the end of the day
    was time
    to be paid
the owner asked everyone
    to sit

he started
    with those
    who had arrived
    in the afternoon
abraham
    returned to his seat
    after being paid
    a full day's wages
saying
    now you jesus
    will surely
    receive two coins
abraham
    was beaming with joy
jesus' name
    was called
    he returned
    with the one coin
now there must
    be something wrong
    thought abraham
        how could they receive
        the same salary?
    he had worked less

abraham
    i saw the owner
    at lunch listening to your story
    his heart was moved
        he was trying
        to be compassionate

abraham and jesus
    walked back together
        tired
        but content
once again
    being with jesus
    it was seen
    how there is a different way
    of being brother and sister
        so all can
        have their needs
        sufficiently met
        every day

a mother's love

(Matthew 15:21–28)

Introduction

In this meditation a gentile woman begs Jesus to heal her daughter. She takes great risks to save her.

The Question

Jesus, do I appreciate those who help me out? I would like to reach out to one person who is physically suffering....

GOSPEL

Leaving that place, Jesus withdrew to the region of Tyre and Sidon. Now a Canaanite woman came from those borders and began to cry out, "Lord, Son of David, have pity on me! My daughter is tormented by a demon." But Jesus did not answer her, not even a word. So his disciples approached him and said, "Send her away: see how she is shouting after us."

Then Jesus said to her, "I was sent only to the lost sheep of the nation of Israel."

But the woman was already kneeling before Jesus and said, "Sir, help me!" Jesus answered, "It is not right to take the bread from the children and throw it to the little dogs." The woman replied, "It is true, sir, but even the little dogs eat the crumbs which fall from their master's table."

Then Jesus said, "Woman, how great is your faith! Let it be as you wish." And her daughter was healed at that moment.

Meditation

rebecca
> all her life
> had wanted a child
>> four years
>> of being married
>> no offspring

her friends
> with their babies
> stopped
> visiting her

even her family
> started to treat
> rebecca differently

she started to feel
> more and more
> apart

she would go to bed
> at night
> thinking
> about being
> a mother

how could god
> punish her
> so severely
> painfully

then it happened
> as quickly
> as unexpectedly
> as the brightest shooting star
>> she was pregnant

the happiest days
 of her life
 when she held
 her daughter
 in her arms
being a mother
 never did rebecca
 think
 she could be so happy
walking
 to the well
 with her daughter
 a love started to flow
  so deeply
she truly loved
 her husband
  she had been fortunate
 but the love
 she felt for her daughter
 was something special
  only a parent
  would understand
 it was as if
 a dance had begun
 in her heart
  because of this
  her heart beat
  differently
her daughter
 grew
 into a beautiful girl

then as suddenly
    as she found out
    she was pregnant
        her daughter
        was overtaken
        by a darkness
        so strong
        she lost who
        she was
this pain
    tore into her heart
    ripped her into pieces
rebecca lost her appetite
    she was desperate
    would do anything
    to regain her daughter
her neighbors
    told her about
    this healer from nazareth
he would be visiting
    her town
she was ready
    to try anything
walking to the plaza
    it was hot
she saw the crowd
    all her life
    she had been reserved
        but her despair
        drove her hurriedly
        to the head
        of the crowd

rebecca finally
 caught sight of jesus
 he was sitting down
 by the well
 resting after speaking
she seized
 the moment
the love for susana
 this love of a mother
  thrust her
  in front of jesus
master
 i know
 i do not share your religion
 i know
  but many
  have told me
  you have a heart
  like light gentle rain
  accepting
  loving
could you help me
 with a request?
i didn't come here
 to ask something
 for myself
rather
 jesus
 as a mother
 i love my daughter
 more than anyone
  else in the world

darkness
    is destroying
    everything about her
could you jesus
    help her
    could you heal her?
i have tried
    everything
    everything
        please

large warm
    passionate tears
    flowed down her cheeks
        reflecting
        catching the faces
        of those sitting
        around this one
jesus was moved inside
    but he would act slowly
jesus
    could feel the love
    of this woman
    for her daughter
he decided
    to be silent
he stood up
    to finish a conversation
    of one with a skin disease
rebecca
    went to peter

sir

    i see

    you are one of his disciples

    i will not leave here

    without results

peter

    tried to pull away

    she grasped his cloak

i am not leaving

    until this master

    grants my request

i won't leave

        i won't

peter realized

    the love of this woman

    for her daughter

    was so strong

    she wasn't going away

        easily

he wanted

    to get rid of her

        quickly

peter

    approached

    jesus

jesus

    i know

    this woman is a gentile

    her daughter

    needs help

could you just help her
so we could
>   get rid of her

jesus
>   thought
>   of so many mothers
>   and their love
>   for their children

jesus
>   went back
>   to the bench

sitting down
>   they began
>   to speak

jesus
>   don't dismiss me
>   you need
>   to take care
>   of some of us
>   that don't belong
>   >   please
>   >   help my daughter
>   >   >   help her
>   >   >   please

with this request
>   a thousand voices
>   vibrated
>   around the circle
>   >   in this plaza

all those
    who love passionately their children
    whose heart is broken
        by watching them suffer
rebecca
    had felt so powerless
    watching
    her daughter suffer
these voices
    vibrated
    in the plaza
    all those who love
        so much
    who are passionate
    who have committed
    so profoundly
    with another person
jesus
    could hear these voices
jesus
    thought of those
        in his own life
        who meant so much
    their faces
    passed through his heart
jesus
    taking rebecca's hand
    lifting her to the bench
        what is your daughter's name?
at this
    relief spread
    over the disciples' faces

we will finally be able
    to get rid
    of this woman
we knew
    she would not go away
    till
    jesus helped her

jesus
    my daughter's name
    is susana
        tears filling rebecca's eyes
jesus
    all my life
    i wanted a daughter
finally
    god blessed me
but two months ago
    a darkness took over

jesus
    looked into her eyes
    seeing a love
    only a mother has
a love so strong
    she has broken
    all customs
    to be sitting
        next to him
jesus
    could also feel
    in her eyes

how much pain
not only the tears
spoke of this
but the dark circles
around her eyes
the lines
across her face
jesus
thinking
in that moment
of his own mother
his heart skipped a beat
jesus
reaches out
he puts his hand
over her head
praying
god
you have taught me
to love
i ask you now
to take away
all the darkness
that inhabits
her daughter
may she continue
to love her
for she has shown us
that to be a mother
to love a child
tenderly

    is truly
    god
    what delights
        your heart
    what lights up
        your face

jesus
    looking
        about him
seeing
    so many mothers
    holding their children
jesus
    was glad
    he could help rebecca

your daughter is cured
    because
    rebecca
        you truly
        have loved much

an intense light
    shot through her
    her request
    had been granted
jumping up
    jesus thank you
        i will never
        be able to thank you
        enough

rebecca
    ran by all the mothers
    with their babies
    walking around
        the plaza
she ran
    as quickly
        as her feet
        would permit her
    to her home
she opened the door
    she peered
    at the table
    her daughter
        nothing could compare
        to the love
            the love exploding
            in her heart
she ran up
    to her daughter
    tears
    falling down
    her face
        swiftly
susana

mama
    where have you been?
i feel
    like i just have woken up
    from a long sleep

mother and daughter
    a love intertwined
this day with jesus
    changed their lives

the days
    passed quickly
    in their lives
rebecca
    never
    forgot those moments
    with jesus
jesus
    also remembered rebecca
    that night
    talking
    with his friends
    around the fire
        speaking
        of how he was moved
        by the gentile woman
        who loved so much
how good it is
    to be passionate
    about life
a passion
    that pushes
    through the veins
        so strongly
        that you push
        in front of a crowd

as a woman
a gentile
but in love
with your child
how good it was for me
to feel such passion
such love
what a good mother
rebecca is
friends
let us learn
from this one
where we perhaps
might not expect
to find a message
i know
you all thought
she was too pushy
and she was
but because
she loves so much
it is time now
to sleep
let us ask ourselves
how
and whom
we love so much
good night

the stars studded
across the sky

a banquet for all

(Matthew 22:1–12)

Introduction

In this meditation we see that Jesus and his friends liked to be by the water. Perhaps one evening as they walked along the shore they were invited by Jacob, the owner of a large house, to help out at a grand banquet. Jesus and his disciples come with their talents, talents to work hard on putting on a party with their music and cooking instruments.

The Question

I see in my own life that I have become secure with whom I eat. Jesus, in what concrete way can I step out of my security and eat sometimes with those people I feel insecure with?

GOSPEL

Jesus went on speaking to them in parables: "This story throws light on the kingdom of heaven. A king celebrated the wedding of his son. He sent his servants to call the invited guests to the wedding feast, but the guests refused to come.

"Again he sent other servants ordering them to say to the invited guests: 'I have prepared a banquet, slaughtered my fattened calves and other animals, and now everything is ready; come then, to the wedding feast.' But they paid no attention and went away, some to their fields, and others to their work. While the rest seized the servants of the king, insulted them and killed them.

"The king became angry. He sent his troops to destroy those murderers and burn their city. Then he said to his servants: 'The wedding banquet is prepared, but the invited guests were not worthy. Go, then, to the crossroads and invite everyone you find to the wedding feast.'

"The servants went out at once into the streets and gathered everyone they found, good and bad alike, so that the hall was filled with guests."

Meditation

the house by the lake
    stood out
    its view was overpowering
        so easy to watch the sun
        drop behind the mountains
jacob the owner of this house
    was the best doctor
    in caphernaum
we were walking
    along the shore
jacob inviting us
    to help him with his party
this very evening
    he was inviting
    all the important people
    of the city
jacob had a good heart
    he helped us
    sometimes
we brought our musical instruments
    to play at the dance

we brought our hands
    ready to help make this
    a good event
it was five o'clock
    the sun would be setting
    at six
messengers started to arrive
    their masters
    were very busy tonight
        sorry but they send regrets
another messenger arriving
    sorry but his master
    is taking a trip
we had prepared three lambs
    the smells invigorated
    the afternoon air
jesus
    sat down next
    to jacob
    whose face
    reflected sadness
        anxiety
why aren't any
    of those invited
    coming?
        all too busy
        with their excuses

jacob
    jesus said
        look at all this food
        you cannot waste it

jesus
pointing to the poor part
of caphernaum
    why don't you invite
    those who have been following us
    they won't let you down

but jesus
    i have never
    walked in that part
    of town

jesus
    grabbing his cloak
        let's go
    walking down the steepest
    street
        invite those here
    they were two men
    living in tents

walking further on
    jesus knocked
    on the door
    at the end of the street
        a woman
            whose world
            was dark
            whose vision
            had been blocked
        she recognized jesus' voice
        she joined our group

we passed two prostitutes
    exhausted
    half asleep
        inviting them also
we stopped by where
    the homeless sleep
jesus found three still awake
    they could not walk
    very well
        so we assisted them
we made our way
    slowly
    being joined by others
        even the motley street children
        had joined us

all those who supposedly
    were too busy
    to come to the party
    suddenly appeared
gazing down on us
    from their balconies
    as we passed
ridiculing us
    but i secretly think
    they were jealous
        we were having
        too much fun

when we arrived
    at jacob's house
    the sun had set

breeze off the lake
the stars were appearing
the food was ready
i sat with jesus around a table
    with maria
        a prostitute
    with tobias
    lazarus
        two street children
    with daniel
        who had a skin disease
    with susana
        who was partially crippled
the candles
    from the middle of the table
    cast light on their joyful faces
maria asking
    if this is what
    the kingdom of god
    is going to be like

who would have ever thought
    we would be sitting here
    in such wonderful company
    enjoying such a delicious meal
    overlooking the lake?
jesus looked at maria
    maria did you know
    that jacob invited
    all those who live
    around here?
        none of them could make it

they live isolated
    from each other
i saw some
    of them watching us
how many times
    have i tried to speak
    to their hearts
        but could not reach them
    they are so self-reliant
but everyone here tonight
    knows
    they can never make it
    on their own
tonight my friends
    jesus smiling at maria
    we are celebrating
        how we are at a banquet
        celebrating
        the kingdom of god
very different
    from other banquets
    where only the pure dine

jesus
    looked about him
    his heart was full
        the stars ever brighter
        the music began
the rejected of society
    those who live hidden
    isolated from the decent
        pushed back their chairs

they helped
    each other up
if i had not been there
    i could never
    have believed it
there was a tenderness
    a care shown
    as they moved
    to the musical chords
        filling the night
it was
    as if for this brief moment
    they could really taste
    what it is
    to be participating
    in god's banquet
        where who they are
        is valued
they enjoyed the music
    and each other's company
    until the sun came up

jacob never again
    had a party
    with those he normally invited
that night changed him
    he was no longer
    a stranger
    to where the rejected lived
he now shares meals
     in their homes

every year
    on the same day
    he invites them
    to return to his house
    to celebrate
        belonging to god's kingdom
jacob
    that night at the banquet
    had never seen such happiness

who enters first?

(Matthew 21:28–32)

Introduction

In this meditation Jesus and his friends arrive late one night to Jerusalem. They are hungry. Nearby the walls of Jerusalem some prostitutes are cooking. They invite Jesus and his friends to eat with them.

The Question

Jesus, sometimes I am judgmental toward others without really knowing what is going on within them. Who is someone in my own life whom I have judged harshly?

GOSPEL

Jesus went on to say, "What do you think of this? A man had two sons. He went to the first and said to him: 'Son, today go and work in my vineyard.' And the son answered: 'I don't want to.' But later he thought better of it and went. Then the father went to the second and gave him the same command. This son replied: 'I will go, sir,' but he did not go. Which of the two did what the father wanted?"

They answered, "The first."

And Jesus said to them, "Truly, I say to you: the publicans and the prostitutes are ahead of you on the way to the kingdom of heaven. For John came to show you the way of goodness but you did not believe him, yet the publicans and the prostitutes did. You were witnesses of this, but you neither repented nor believed him."

Meditation

once again it was time
    for the high holy days
so many pilgrims
    journeying for so many days
we had arrived late
    camping
    outside the gates tonight

jesus and i
    went looking for food
    but we were late
fires being lit everywhere
    people settling in for the night
so hungry

nearby were the prostitutes
    they were preparing food
    before a long night
        the meat smelled
        so delicious
i went with jesus
    to their campsite
veronica the leader
    told us
    not to worry about it
    there was plenty
    for everyone

our whole group
    wandered over
    around the fire
        soon enjoying the food
        and the company of these women
veronica started
    to tell us her story
she was now twenty-two
    she'd been working in this profession
    for six years
jesus asked her
    what were her dreams
veronica stood up
    she waved her hands
        to have a house
        for her two children
        a small clothes business
but this was only a dream
    she felt
    her destiny had condemned her
    to this kind of work
there was a kindness
    goodness
    within veronica
    that jesus was drawing out

you could feel
    how difficult life
    was for these women
but they seemed to take care
    of each other

suddenly
    arriving in front of us
    five of the well-known pharisees
they looked at us
    with such judgment
        i felt dirty
        condemned
        just by sitting here
i will never
    forget that scene
        our group eating
        conversing
        with the prostitutes
    right above
        these pharisees
the senior among them
    stepped forward
jesus i imagine
    you and your friends
    have no idea
    with whom
    you are sharing a meal
his self-righteousness
    his disdain
    had created
    an uneasiness
    among these women
veronica
    stood up
she was not going
    to be put down

holy one ephieus
 these friends were hungry
 we shared our food
  leave them alone
and ephieus
 if i remember correctly
 you have a large black mole
  on your back

outrage swept across his face

ephieus you know
 what i mean
  one of my girls
  pointed you out
  last week
 she spoke about your birthmark
you pretend to be so holy
  so pure
 but you are dishonest
we are what we are
 prostitutes
we don't march
 down the aisles of the temple
 pretending to be so clean
  so holy

ephieus looked at the other
 four pharisees
i do not know
 what this crazy woman
 is talking about

you know my pious wife
we are so happy together

his lie was dripping
from his mouth
there was no truth
found in ephieus
veronica asked simply
ephieus can you ever be honest?
how hard
it must be
to always be pretending
fooling yourself
fooling everyone else
do you even know
who you are?

ephieus
screaming
you wretch
shut your mouth

the night listened

veronica
a radiance all across her face
no ephieus
all my life
i have been told
to be quiet
that i am no good
worthless

but this preacher here
has let me see
i no longer
want to be
stepped upon
by men like you
you lie to your wife
to the world
i won't be silent any longer
i will speak the truth
we are meant
to all live together
as brothers and sisters
ephieus
tonight i really wonder
who the pure
and the impure are

all the women
stood up
music filled the air
with the presence
of these broken
vulnerable prostitutes

the walls around the city
shook
even the massive structure
of the temple
moved its foundation
in the silence
of the night

it was as if
    all the pilgrims
    heard the whispering
        of these voices:
how dare you pharisees
religious leaders
        judge us
        condemn us
        the outcasts
our god loves us
    loves us so much
    that we can feel
    our goodness
we share our food
    we help each other
        in times of need
we dream someday
    we won't be forced
    to work like we do

it was eleven o'clock
    the pharisees slipped
    back into the dark untruth
        of their night
the fire was low
    veronica
    came and sat
    next to jesus
        her long hair
        blown by the night breeze
jesus
    i have been thinking

have learned something
        tonight
have listened
        as you explained
        about
        the kingdom of god
is there a place
for people like us?

jesus
        i would like
        to join your group
        know things
        will work out

jesus
        not saying anything
        smiling
once again
        experiencing
        who are the spiritual people
        of this land
how god
        you are hidden
        where we least
        expect
        to find you

jesus' heart was joyful
        to feel
        his god
        so close

learned something
    about jesus that night
    outside the city wall
        he was so accepting
        of everyone we met
i think
    i became a better friend
    of his
    after this
the tenderness i felt
    in his heart
    moved me
        i wanted to become
        like this
with jesus
    there were always
    surprises
before knowing jesus
    i could never imagine myself
    sitting around a campfire
        sharing a meal
    with prostitutes
but that was jesus
    always expanding our vision
    of where his god
        dwells

what is most important?

(Matthew 25:31–46)

Introduction

In this meditation we see that as people of faith sometimes it is easy to get distracted from what Jesus asks us to do. It is easy to be so busy about so many things that we forget what really is important.

The Question

I see in my own life that sometimes I have forgotten your invitation to follow you. Jesus, how could I follow you more closely by doing one concrete action?

GOSPEL

"When the Son of Man comes in his glory with all his angels, he will sit on the throne of his Glory. All the nations will be brought before him, and as a shepherd separates the sheep from the goats, so will he do with them, placing the sheep on his right and the goats on his left.

"The King will say to those on his right: 'Come, blessed of my Father! Take possession of the kingdom prepared for you from the beginning of the world. For I was hungry and you fed me, I was thirsty and you gave me drink. I was a stranger and you welcomed me into your house. I was naked and you clothed me. I was sick and you visited me. I was in prison and you came to see me.'

117

"Then the good people will ask him: 'Lord, when did we see you hungry and give you food, thirsty and give you drink, or a stranger and welcome you, or naked and clothe you? When did we see you sick or in prison and go to see you?' The King will answer, 'Truly, I say to you: whenever you did this to these little ones who are my brothers and sisters, you did it to me.'

"Then he will say to those on his left: 'Go, cursed people, out of my sight into the eternal fire which has been prepared for the devil and his angels! For I was hungry and you did not give me anything to eat, I was thirsty and you gave me nothing to drink; I was a stranger and you did not welcome me into your house; I was naked and you did not clothe me; I was sick and in prison and you did not visit me.'

"They, too, will ask: 'Lord, when did we see you hungry, thirsty, naked or a stranger, sick or in prison, and did not help you?' The King will answer them: 'Truly, I say to you: whatever you did not do for one of these little ones, you did not do for me.' And these will go into eternal punishment, but the just to eternal life."

Meditation

the curtains had been drawn
    everyone gathered in the stadium
    everyone waiting for jesus to arrive
all morning long
    everyone had sat
    answering questions
    difficult beyond belief
        if your parish council
        wants to get rid
        of your pastor
        because he is a poor preacher
            what would you do?

if there is only enough money
to pay a choir director
or a secretary
    what would you do?
if you are hiring
a new religious education coordinator
the latina is more culturally sensitive
to the needs of the congregation
plus she can communicate
with the whole parish
the irish nun however
has years of experience
and a deep love for the poor
but her spanish is medium
    who would you pick?
all morning long
    these faithful followers of jesus
    remembered back
    to the trial tests
    that u.c.l.a. had prepared for them
this test they took
    would decide everything
all their years of faithful service
    would be judged by this test
jesus
    had the test scores
    in his hands
as he came before the microphone
    a silence settled over the crowd
at that moment
    a youth of eighteen years
    stood up

jesus
>i have a question
>for you

everyone wondered
>what could be happening
>>how at this decisive moment
>>could someone ask a question

jesus
>there is a serious problem here
i don't think your god
>cares about the answers
>to these questions
>the way we took the test
i look at all of us
>we are so sophisticated
>with our religious language
>worrying about certain
>preserving of structures
>>ways that the prophets of old
>>denounced so strongly
we worry
>are so preoccupied
>about so many concerns
jesus
>during the test
>i looked up
>and saw a brother immigrant
>near the podium
i went up to him
>he had just crossed the border

he was hungry
 i took him to a hamburger stand
 and bought him
 a hamburger
his name is enrique
 he had a bible
 he opened it
 tore out this page
i read it
 tears ran down my face
all the hours in committee meetings
 all the hours spent in planning
 looking at priorities
 studies and more studies
this young man
 enrique
 gave me this page
 which says
 i was hungry
 you fed me
 i was thirsty
 you gave me to drink
 i was a stranger
 you gave me hospitality
 i was naked
 you clothed me
 i was sick
 you accompanied me
 i was in prison
 you visited me
in that one instant at the hamburger stand
 with this brother

    i saw so clearly
    the answers to all the questions
    of this difficult examination
the moment we get distracted
    from these six descriptions
    of where we find god
        we lose
        we have already failed
i don't think
    any of us
    passed this test
jesus
    here is the answer
    to my exam

this youth joseph
    walked up to jesus
    and handed him
    the page
    with these six answers
    hunger
        thirst
    hospitality
        solidarity
    sickness
        imprisoned
jesus smiled
    he invited enrique
    to come
    before the crowd
jesus asked enrique
    to tell his story

there was not a dry eye
    in the stadium
    when he finished telling
    how he had five children
    lived on a small farm
one day robbers
    entered their household
    stole all his belongings
could not buy seed
    to plant his parcel
    to have a crop
        his only source
        of income
he started to see
    his children go hungry
    his three-month-old baby died
        his heart was broken
            torn apart
then his wife got sick
    almost died
    she would need medication
    for the rest of her life
he risked his life
    so many times
    trying to cross the border
finally arriving in los angeles
    he needed to earn enough
    by the end of each month
    or she would die
everyone's eyes watered silently
    the suffering of this immigrant
        without resources

now
    jesus said
    i want you to go back
    and answer these questions
    all of you
    and let enrique's story
    roll around in you
remembering
    israel as an enslaved people
        oppressed by the egyptians
    cried out to god
        they were liberated
those who were most defenseless
        most vulnerable
        are favored in god's eyes
the moment
    our vision is not connected
    to being with those
    who are most oppressed
    we are worshiping
    the golden idols
    of the egyptians
there was a lightness
    about those who returned
    to take the exam
they could answer easily now
they let their hearts
    enter into the process
the story of enrique
    and the millions like him
        were present

everyone easily passed the exam
    so grateful
    that they invited enrique
    to stay with them
    because they all knew
    they would have failed
        this exam
        miserably
        if enrique
        had not appeared

unconditional love

(Mark 2:23–28)

Introduction

In this meditation we meet Jesus and his friends having a day in the country. They are hungry. In this relaxing setting Peter reflects back on how he has felt judged, put down because his family was considered outcasts by society.

The Question

Jesus, do I really believe I am unconditionally loved by you? I remember this one time when I experienced your overwhelming love...

GOSPEL

One sabbath he was walking through grainfields. As his disciples walked along with him, they began to pick the heads of grain and crush them in their hands. Then the Pharisees said to Jesus, "Look! they are doing what is forbidden on the sabbath!"

And he said to them, "Have you never read what David did in his time of need, when he and his men were very hungry? He went into the house of God when Abiathar was High Priest and ate the bread of offering, which only the priests are allowed to eat, and he also gave some to the men who were with him."

Then Jesus said to them, "The sabbath was made for man, not man for the sabbath. So the Son of Man is master even of the sabbath."

Meditation

the fields
    stretched on
    forever
row after row
    of corn
that afternoon
    the wind
    blew through the stalks
a certain music
    was being created
the whole week
    we had been surrounded
    by the sick
    been involved
    in many problems
today
    we had left early
        to rest
        far away
        from everyone
talking about
    how we were probably
    being followed
jesus
    was alive today
    his eyes shined
    catching
        the vastness
        of being
        in the country

jesus
>i am glad
>we are here
>>walking slowly
>>through this field
>it is good to be
>with you

jesus
>that diseased woman yesterday
>she hardly
>>seemed human
>but the way
>>you bent down
>>and prayed for her
>>>healed her

jesus
>what i felt yesterday
>is how much
>you loved her
>>while everyone else
>>scorned her

peter
>my god loves her
>without limits

jesus
>that is what
>we talked about
>>in our group
>>before sleeping
>>last night

how much your god
loves each one of us
    but
    we really don't believe it
we have been taught
    to feel impure
        outside of the
        religious system
    as a result
    it is hard for me
        personally
    to really believe
        i am loved
            by your god
so many years
    of hearing the opposite
    stops me jesus
    from feeling this

jesus' eyes
    pierced into me
        we sat down
        with the view
        of the whole countryside
    some of our group
    were hungry
    and began to eat
    from the stalks
this gave me
    the opportunity
    to spend time
    with jesus

i told him
>how
>ever since
>i could remember
>>i desired to be close
>>to one greater

when i studied
>in the synagogue
>i would be moved
>by how god acted
>>rescuing our people
>>from slavery

felt sometimes
>this presence so strong

i could feel
>one greater
>present with me

but then
>when i was nine
>our family was thrown out
>of the synagogue
>>because my brother
>>had leprosy
>all doors
>were closed to us

that is when
>i began to feel
>how god
>was not pleased with me

we were outcasts
>like so many others

the division
    between the pure and the impure
    became clearer to me
yesterday jesus
    watching you
        the way you touched
        that woman so tortured
        by sickness
    something
    broke open within me
    i wanted
    to free myself
    from this feeling
        of being far away
        from god
was glad my friends
    were somewhat distant
    eating
because these tremendous memories
    rejection
    sadness
    of being told
    i was condemned by god
        were too much
i could not help myself
    i began to weep
sorrow flowing out
    from every part
    of my being
for years
    i had lived
    with this alienation

i never
want to go
back to that place
    of self-hate
what right
does anyone have
to tell us
we are despised by god?
glad
    jesus
you are healing me
of this
by who you are
by what you do
and by whom you choose
to be with
jesus
    embraced me
and once again
i experienced the love
of one greater
    a presence so deep
    so powerful
to be loved
by your god
not to just know it
but to feel it
thank you
    jesus
for letting me experience
this love

just as i finished
    telling jesus all this
    the pharisees
        appeared close to where
        our friends were seated
three of the most arrogant
    the oldest pointing his finger
    at the stalks
    that had been picked
jesus
    holy one
    don't you know
    this is forbidden
    on the sabbath
i had to refrain
    an anger so powerful
    emptied
    from the deepest place
        within
here again
    these so called pure ones
    were throwing us aside
    by their rigorous
        legal system
angry
    how useless outdated laws
        were keeping us
        from god
    how this judgmental
    condemnation
    had made
    so many feel

so dirty
so worthless
never even worthy
to address god
i wanted
to scream at them
how dare
they try to enslave god
god is so much bigger
than their small
judgmental world

peter
stay here
i will approach them
jesus
slowly walking
to where
the three stood
with disdain dripping
from their eyes

friends
good you could find time
to be
in the countryside
it seems
you are upset
at the actions
of my friends
they have worked hard
all week

        we have not stopped
        to eat
    they were starving
of course
    we remember our ancestor david
        when he was starving
        he went into the place
        of worship
    took the bread
    that was reserved
    just for the priests
he brought it
    outside
    sat down
    with his friends
    and shared it
    with them
    just like
    my friends are doing now
perhaps
    this might say
    something
    about who our creator is
laws
    are to protect us
    provide us
    with a way to live together
our creator
    did not desire
    that david starve
    nor does he desire this
        for our group here

laws
>are not meant
>to enslave us

the three listening
>their disgust
>growing with time

i could tell
>from where
>i was seated
>they did not understand
>anything
>that jesus was explaining

they turned their backs
>left abruptly
>as only
>pure self-righteous
>>can do

so many things
>came together
>for me
>that afternoon

jesus
>returned smiling

peter
>you really are free
>and loved
>by one greater

let's continue
>walking
>enjoying
>the beauty of creation

i felt lighter
    i never returned
    to that place
    of feeling alienated
        from god
presence
    overwhelming
    feeling that afternoon
        deep
        overflowing
we enjoyed the whole day
    refreshed
    to begin another week
jesus
    a great traveling companion
    you never knew
        what was going to happen
i was grateful
    for this friend

About the Author and Speakers

The Crossroad Publishing Company received a great gift last spring. At the Los Angeles Religious Education Congress (LAREC), word was getting out that Martin Sheen, the social activist, great film actor, and Emmy Award–winning actor of NBC's *The West Wing,* was about to appear during Fr. Michael Kennedy's presentation on Ignatian spirituality. We knew in advance that Mr. Sheen had planned to be there, but with the hectic schedules of celebrities, one never knows for sure. Mr. Sheen arrived, and with him pandemonium. We thought, "Here comes the celebrity."

Two events utterly overturned our expectations.

First, Mr. Sheen, one of the most recognizable faces in Hollywood, did not play the celebrity. He spoke alongside Fr. Mike as a colleague, a fellow seeker, a person who like everyone else is trying to understand what it means to follow Christ in daily life. Confounding people who had come expecting him to be an angry protester, he spoke with utter grace and openness, even when talking about people with whose policies he disagreed.

Second, somehow we, and everyone, realized how widespread the excitement had become. It was not just for Sheen. It was not just for Fr. Mike, who had developed a wide readership with his three books for Crossroad and a reputation as a generous LAREC speaker who loved to bring people to LAREC from his East Los Angeles Dolores Mission Parish, sign books in colorful ink, and speak at length with any conference participants interested in doing so. Indeed, the energy was everywhere. We saw it with Janne Shirley, a chaplain in the Office of Detention Ministry for the Archdiocese of Los Angeles, whose eyes are like torches shining with the love of Christ. Janne, who narrates this book with Mr. Sheen, had been central to an LA retreat our staff had taken, where we learned about the lives of adolescents serving life sentences. We saw the energy too with the LAREC organizers, who took what might have been the logistical headache of a high-profile event and turned it into a joyous occasion.

Everywhere, everywhere, joy at this idea, so ancient and yet so new, of going back to Jesus, turning our eyes to him so that we can see ourselves in a different way.

Crossroad thanks everyone who has contributed to the present book and the three earlier books by Fr. Mike. And we thank you, our readers. We hope that in your life, *Experiencing Jesus* is rekindling a sense of the power of Jesus to transform, energize, and bring about the unexpected.

ALSO BY MICHAEL KENNEDY, S.J.

THE JESUS MEDITATIONS
A Guide for Contemplation

With accompanying CD read by Martin Sheen

Have you ever longed to walk beside Jesus on the dusty roads of Palestine? Have you ever wondered what it would feel like to be in the crowd when Jesus was healing and preaching? These powerful meditations will help you imagine being right there with Jesus. Entering into the world of these meditations will change forever your relationship with Jesus, with yourself, and with the world around you.

0-8245-1929-9 $19.95 paperback

EYES ON JESUS
A Guide for Contemplation

"An extraordinary and insightful work for personal reflection on the relevance of the gospels to our modern daily lives." — Martin Sheen

Read these poems aloud, and find the Gospels vividly spring to life. Michael Kennedy's words summon a powerful response to Scripture and compel readers to risk engaging Jesus' story in a new way.

0-8245-1828-4, $14.95 paperback

EYES ON THE CROSS
With illustrations by Bernardo Gantier Zelada, S.J.

Written in the tradition of the Spiritual Exercises of St. Ignatius, *Eyes on the Cross* comprises starkly revealing poems that have the power to focus the mind and uplift the heart.

0-8245-1879-9, $14.95 paperback

crossroad

OF RELATED INTEREST

Ronald Rolheiser
THE SHATTERED LANTERN
Rediscovering a Felt Presence of God

The way back to a lively faith "is not a question of finding the right answers, but of living a certain way. The existence of God, like the air we breathe, need not be proven...." Rolheiser shines new light on the contemplative path of Western Christianity and offers a dynamic way forward.

"Whenever I see Ron Rolheiser's name on a book, I know that it will be an amazing combination of true orthodoxy and revolutionary insight — and written in a clear and readable style. He knows the spiritual terrain like few others, and you will be profoundly illuminated by this lantern. Read and be astonished." — Richard Rohr, O.F.M.

0-8245-1884-5, $14.95 paperback

Ronald Rolheiser
AGAINST AN INFINITE HORIZON
The Finger of God in our Everyday Lives

Full of personal anecdotes, healing wisdom, and a fresh reflection on Scripture, *Against an Infinite Horizon* draws on the great traditions of parable and storytelling. In this prequel to the bestseller *The Holy Longing*, Rolheiser's new fans will be delighted with further insights into the benefits of community, social justice, sexuality, mortality, and rediscovering the deep beauty and poetry of Christian spirituality.

"Ronald Rolheiser has mastered the old, old art of parable."
— Morris West

"A felicitous blend of scriptural reflection, shrewd psychological observations, and generous portions of letters sent to Rolheiser and his responses." — *Commonweal*

0-8245-1965-5, $16.95 paperback

crossroad

OF RELATED INTEREST

Richard Rohr
EVERYTHING BELONGS
The Gift of Contemplative Prayer

Revised & Updated!

Richard Rohr has written this book to help us pray better and see life differently. Using parables, koans, and personal experiences, he leads us beyond the techniques of prayer to a place where we can receive the gift of contemplation: the place where (if only for a moment) we see the world in God clearly, and know that everything belongs.

"Rohr at his finest: insightful cultural critique — with strong connection to the marginalized."
— *The Other Side*

A personal retreat for those who hunger for a deeper prayer life but don't know what contemplation really is or how to let it happen.

0-8245-1995-7, $16.95 paperback

Please support your local bookstore,
or call 1-800-707-0670 for Customer Service.

For a free catalog, write us at

THE CROSSROAD PUBLISHING COMPANY
16 Penn Plaza, 481 Eighth Avenue
New York, NY 10001

Visit our website at
www.crossroadpublishing.com
All prices subject to change.

crossroad